Native American
Confederacies

ANNA CAREW-MILLER

Senior Consulting Editor Dr. Troy Johnson
Professor of History and American Indian Studies
California State University

MASON CREST PUBLISHERS • PHILADELPHIA

NATIVE AMERICAN LIFE

NATIVE AMERICAN LIFE

Native American
Confederacies

ANNA CAREW-MILLER

Senior Consulting Editor Dr. Troy Johnson
Professor of History and American Indian Studies
California State University

MASON CREST PUBLISHERS • PHILADELPHIA

NATIVE AMERICAN LIFE

Mason Crest Publishers
370 Reed Road
Broomall, PA 19008
www.masoncrest.com

First printing

1 3 5 7 9 8 6 4 2

Library of Congress Cataloging-in-Publication Data
on file at the Library of Congress

ISBN 1-59084-128-X

Frontispiece: Reenactment of a charge from the 1876 Battle of the Little
Bighorn, during which a confederation of Sioux and Cheyenne warriors
defeated a U.S. cavalry unit commanded by George Armstrong Custer.

Table of Contents

Introduction

For hundreds of years the dominant image of the Native American has been that of a stoic warrior, often wearing a full-length eagle feather headdress, riding a horse in pursuit of the buffalo, or perhaps surrounding some unfortunate wagon train filled with innocent west-bound American settlers. Unfortunately there has been little written or made available to the general public to dispel this erroneous generalization. This misrepresentation has resulted in an image of native people that has been translated into books, movies, and television programs that have done little to look deeply into the native worldview, cosmology, and daily life. Not until the 1990 movie *Dances with Wolves* were native people portrayed as having a human persona. For the first time, native people could express humor, sorrow, love, hate, peace, and warfare. For the first time native people could express themselves in words other than "ugh" or "Yes, Kemo Sabe." This series has been written to provide a more accurate and encompassing journey into the world of the Native Americans.

When studying the native world of the Americas, it is extremely important to understand that there are few "universals" that apply across tribal boundaries. With over 500 nations and 300 language groups the worlds of the Native Americans were diverse. The traditions of one group may or may not have been shared by neighboring groups. Sports, games, dance, subsistence patterns, clothing, and religion differed—greatly in some instances. And although nearly all native groups observed festivals and ceremonies necessary to insure the renewal of their worlds, these too varied greatly.

Of equal importance to the breaking down of old myopic and stereotypic images is that the authors in this series credit Native

Americans with a sense of agency. Contrary to the views held by the Europeans who came to North and South America and established the United States, Canada, Mexico, and other nations, some Native American tribes had sophisticated political and governing structures— that of the member nations of the Iroquois League, for example. Europeans at first denied that native people had religions but rather "worshiped the devil," and demanded that Native Americans abandon their religions for the Christian worldview. The readers of this series will learn that native people had well-established religions, led by both men and women, long before the European invasion began in the 16th and 17th centuries.

Gender roles also come under scrutiny in this series. European settlers in the northeastern area of the present-day United States found it appalling that native women were "treated as drudges" and forced to do the men's work in the agricultural fields. They failed to understand, as the reader will see, that among this group the women owned the fields and scheduled the harvests. Europeans also failed to understand that Iroquois men were diplomats and controlled over one million square miles of fur-trapping area. While Iroquois men sat at the governing council, Iroquois clan matrons caucused with tribal members and told the men how to vote.

These are small examples of the material contained in this important series. The reader is encouraged to use the extended bibliographies provided with each book to expand his or her area of specific interest.

Dr. Troy Johnson
Professor of History and American Indian Studies
California State University

Native Americans beat a drum at a gathering in modern-day Alberta, Canada. Today, Native American tribes are understood as political and cultural groupings of peoples. In the past, a tribe was a group of people who were bound by blood ties, lived together in a defined area, and spoke the same language.

1 Native American Confederacies

Among Native Americans, a **confederacy** was an **alliance** formed between tribes. In order to understand why and how confederacies were formed, it is important to understand what a tribe is. Today, Native American tribes are understood both as political groupings and as cultural groupings of peoples. However, in the past, a tribe was a group of **indigenous** people bound by blood ties, with their own rules for society, religion, and politics, who lived together in a defined area and spoke a common language.

The organizations that we know today as tribes were mostly created after contact with Europeans and the disease and disruption that came with them. Before contact, ancient America was populated by groups of people who were connected by common rituals and beliefs. These groups of people felt united by a common identity, but this identity shifted and changed over time for a number of reasons, including the availability of food resources in their homeland, lifestyle innovations (such as the introduction of the horse), and relationships with neighboring tribes. Tribes, and their relationships to other tribes, were constantly evolving.

Many confederacies, or groups of tribes who worked together, were created as a result of European contact. These tribes united

The Wappinger Confederacy made a well-known trade with Dutch colonists. For some cheap trinkets, said to be worth $24, they traded a portion of their territory—what is now known as Manhattan Island. However, perhaps the Wappinger felt that they were getting the better part of the deal: They did not believe they had given up possession of this land, because they did not believe anyone could own it.

against a common enemy. However, there may have been confederacies prior to European contact as well. Archaeological evidence suggests that an ancient confederacy may have been what created the Chacoan culture, which existed in northern New Mexico from about A.D. 950–1100, although the reason for this confederacy during this time remains a mystery. These people flourished in the high desert for a couple hundred years, building adobe structures and temples, but then disappeared. It is thought that a terrible drought brought an end to this gathering of peoples and urban-style culture.

Another complex society that seems also to have involved a confederacy of separate bands of native peoples is that of the Mound Builders, who lived near the Mississippi River. They lived in walled towns and villages under the leadership of a strong chief. This culture flourished from about A.D. 900–1600, and had started to break down before the Spanish conquistadors arrived. After the Spanish conquest of the Southeast, Mississippian culture completely collapsed. However, anthropologists believe that remnants of belief and social customs survived in the tribes that emerged afterward, such as the Creeks.

After the Europeans came, the social and political organization of Native Americans changed, too. Europeans brought diseases with them, diseases that native peoples had little resistance to, if any. Often, long before a tribe had actual contact with any European people, its members had been introduced to a European disease that killed many

Native American woman with a peace pipe, South Dakota.

"How the Indians make Their Alliances and Marriages with Each Other," from a late-16th-century French manuscript. Before the arrival of Europeans in the New World, large alliances among tribes were relatively rare.

of them. Such a loss caused tribes, clans, and bands of native people to reorganize. Then, when the Europeans came, hostility led to bloodshed, and further loss of native peoples caused tribes to reorganize again.

In most regions of the country, separate native tribes became confederacies banded together to deal with a new enemy. In the past, some tribes had worked together to maintain their territory and fight off other, more powerful tribes. However, with the coming of the Europeans, native peoples had to face a new kind of power and way of thinking about land and its possession. Native Americans did not think that they could, as an individual or a tribe, own the land they lived on, whereas the Europeans thought of land as a possession. These newcomers wanted to know who owned the land of the New World and with whom they should negotiate to possess it themselves.

Beginning in the 16th century, Native American tribes had to negotiate and decide who they were in relation to other tribes and the territory they occupied. The formation of alliances and confederacies that did not exist before colonial settlement allowed native peoples, for a time, to face the power of the Europeans. However, there were different groups of Europeans—the French, the Dutch, the English, and the Spanish—to deal with.

Some of the most powerful confederations often became mixed up with European interests and alliances. For example, the Creek Confederacy attempted to use their alliance with the English against the threat of colonial settlers pouring into their territory. On the other hand, the Iroquois League tried to remain neutral as the English and French grew increasingly hostile toward each other in the 18th century.

Many confederacies used the strength of united tribal forces rather than face the European powers alone. They drew on old alliances and reorganized to form new ones to hold back the tide of Europeans coming into their world. A group of smaller tribes formed the Wappinger Confederacy in response to the Dutch coming into their territory, which spread along the east bank of the Hudson River to the tip of what is now Manhattan, to Poughkeepsie and into western Connecticut. Early in the 17th century, this confederacy had nearly 5,000 members. The power of the Wappinger Confederacy broke, however, after a war with the Dutch in the 1640s. The survivors joined more-powerful neighboring tribes.

In the West, a similar reorganization among native peoples took place. In the 1600s, the leaders of the Chumash people on the California coast created a political system enabling them to deal with the Spanish as a unified people. Previously, the Chumash had lived as independent bands, based on clans and extended families. Once the Spanish arrived, the Chumash created a council uniting all the separate groups. The council was an assembly of 20 leaders, including heads of families and *shamans*, and was led by one leader. This system worked while Chumash lived in *dispersed* communities. However, when the tribe moved into the Spanish missions, diseases wiped them out.

The 18th century was an important period for Native American

Powhatan was a powerful chief who is most often remembered today as the father of Pocahontas. When Europeans arrived in what is now Virginia, they saw Powhatan's control of tribes in the Tidewater region and assumed this diverse group of native peoples was a confederacy. However, Powhatan had forced the other tribes to submit to his control through conquest and intimidation; there was no agreement that had caused these tribes to unite.

confederacies, as it was a time of *treaties* with Europeans. The big treaty issue was trade, not the loss of lands, which was more of an issue in the 17th and 19th centuries. The American Revolution was a disaster for the powerful confederacies, such as the Iroquois and the Creek, as it became impossible for these confederacies to fight the unified power of the United States.

15

In the 19th century, many of the old confederacies fell apart. As tribes from the east coast of the United States were pushed west, competition for land, as well as disease and violence, led to political reorganization among tribal groups. As the settlement of the United States moved westward, new confederacies rose and fell as the face of the wilderness changed. Only in the 20th century would new confederacies give Native American peoples power and a voice in the political landscape of the United States. 𝕊

NATIVE AMERICAN LIFE

A modern Iroquois man stands outside a
reconstructed longhouse, his people's
traditional dwelling. The Iroquois League,
which originally consisted of five
Northeastern tribes, was one of the most
powerful Native American confederacies.

2 The Northeast: The Iroquois League

One of the oldest and most powerful confederacies ever formed among native peoples was the Iroquois League. This confederacy was based on internal peace and shared beliefs of respect for ancestors, warriors, and clan mothers. Its people spoke five different *dialects* and belonged to five different tribes: Onondaga, Cayuga, Oneida, Mohawk, and Seneca. They lived in more than 200 villages in what is now upper New York and southern Ontario. They called themselves the People of the Long House, or *Hodenosaunee*, because of the style of structure in which their **matriarchal**, extended families lived.

The Iroquois League was formed around 1450, according to oral histories. These stories explain that before the League was formed, there was a period of constant bloodshed and war among the tribes of this region. The many battles among this warrior people began to have an impact on population and culture. This worried some wise men in these tribes.

The founders of this famous confederacy were two men, Hayenwatha, an Onondaga leader and **orator**, and Deganawidah, a Huron prophet known as the Peacemaker. Deganawidah had a vision.

He believed that these warring peoples must unite under the roots of the Great Tree of Peace, a tall pine tree. He believed that they must live in harmony and justice by forming a government of the law. Deganawidah wanted to end abuses against human beings.

> Oral tradition explains that Hayenwatha started the custom of the *wampum* belt as a negotiating tool. It was a string of shells, which represented a chain of connection between the five tribes.

According to the oral histories, the Peacemaker said: "The white roots of the Great Tree of Peace will continue to grow, advancing the Good Mind and Righteousness and Peace, moving into territories of people scattered far through the forest." The pine tree, with its spreading roots, represented a unified society.

Before he met the Peacemaker, Hayenwatha (sometimes spelled Hiawatha) was a tribal leader struggling to reform his tribe. He had an enemy within the tribe, Tadadaho, who, it is said, was responsible for the death of three of Hayenwatha's daughters. In his grief over his dead daughters, Hayenwatha lost hope; however, meeting the Peacemaker made him believe that thinking could replace violence. Together, the two men traveled from village to village with their message of brotherhood and equality among the tribes. Eventually, all five tribes agreed to accept this idea.

How did the Iroquois League work? It was an early form of *democratic* representative government, which balanced local interests with those of the League as a whole. Their territory was a rectangle covering the area from the Hudson River to Lake Erie. This was further divided into five 200-mile-long north-south strips, each governed by its own tribal council. The senior women chose men to represent their clans at village councils. Each tribe of the League lived in towns and villages,

Hiawatha grieves over the loss of one of his daughters in an illustration from *The Song of Hiawatha*, an 1855 book by Henry Wadsworth Longfellow. The real Hiawatha (also spelled Hayenwatha) cofounded the Iroquois League, which united the Mohawk, Onondaga, Cayuga, Oneida, and Seneca tribes.

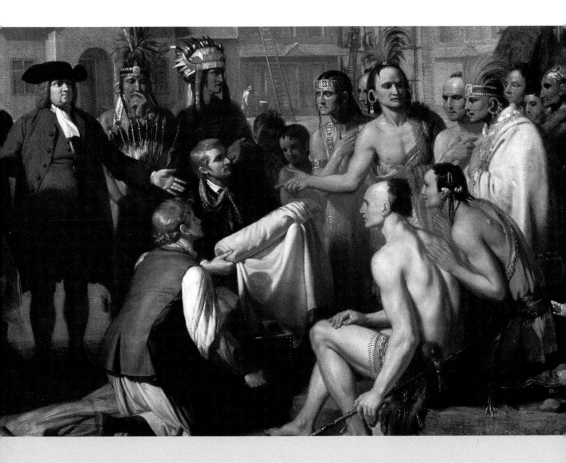

William Penn (far left) concludes a treaty with the Indians in this 18th-century painting. Pressure by whites to settle on their lands spurred many individual tribes to band together into confederacies.

which were independent. The League council did not interfere with affairs of individual tribes.

It was decided that the Onondaga tribe would be the "fire keepers." This meant that they maintained the symbolic fire around which the council met. All the League's great councils were held in an

Onondaga village because they were the most centrally located in the territory. The senior women also chose 49 council chiefs who met with the League as a whole. These tribal representatives made all council decisions unanimously. The council met usually every summer, although the law said it had to meet only once every five years.

For almost 200 years, the Iroquois League existed for peace, not war. Only on rare occasions did the League unite all five tribes to fight an external enemy. However, with the coming of the Europeans, that began to change. After European contact, the League's neutrality was not perfect. Groups of warriors, or even whole tribes, would sometimes fight the English or the French.

By the end of the 18th century, the Iroquois League claimed about 16,000 members, which made it a powerful force for the Europeans to deal with. However, like other tribes, the League suffered because of European diseases.

To combat this and increase their numbers again, their culture believed in replacing dead family members by adopting captive members of enemy tribes, which was also a way of dealing with grief. In addition, the League's numbers grew as remnants of tribes destroyed by disease or conquest were also adopted into the five tribes of the League. In 1722, the Tuscarora tribe joined the Iroquois League after being pushed out of North Carolina by English colonials, becoming the sixth member.

Because of its numbers and its tradition of working together, the League became the critical Indian group in the imperial wars of the 18th century. During the 17th and 18th centuries, the League

21

NATIVE AMERICAN LIFE

It is thought that the democratic ideals and representative government of the Iroquois League influenced Ben Franklin and the writers of the U.S. Constitution.

presented a powerful united front in the face of European conquest. The English and French both believed that this confederacy held the balance of power, and both tried to make alliances with the League.

During this time, the Iroquois closed their lands in New York to armies and war parties of the French and their Indian allies, so the French could not attack New England. This tactic earned them the support of the English. However, the French kept trying to win over the Iroquois, which created a strong pro-French faction within the League. Staying neutral and finding agreement within council meetings became more and more difficult.

In the mid-18th century, the Iroquois broke their neutrality and made a treaty with the English, giving away lands that were the territory of the Delaware, one of the tribes who depended on the League's protection. The Delaware had been part of the Covenant Chain, a league of peace and friendship between the Iroquois and other groups, including the English. This betrayal caused many other tribes to distrust the power of the League. The French soon found many allies among tribes who were happy to see the Iroquois challenged.

The supremacy of the Iroquois League in the Northeast ended with the American Revolution. This war weakened the League because the governing council had refused to take sides. Individual tribes joined the English, except the Oneida, who joined the colonials. The victorious American government treated the Iroquois League as a defeated enemy at the war's end. As a result, they lost control of much of their territory and, more important, their power as a confederacy.

However, the Iroquois League did not disappear. Its remnants survived on small reservations into the 19th century. Today, the League is called the Iroquois Nation, and it is one of the strongest tribal organizations in the Northeast, dedicated to preserving its members' cultural heritage and protecting the civil rights of native peoples. ⑨

23

An Iroquois warrior scalps a white man in this late-18th-century French illustration. Both Great Britain and France courted the powerful Iroquois League, which eventually allied itself with Britain.

NATIVE AMERICAN LIFE

In the winter of 1838-39, the Cherokee tribe, part of the Creek Confederacy, was forced from its land in Georgia and Alabama and relocated in Indian Territory (in present-day Oklahoma). During the grueling journey, known as the Trail of Tears, about one-third of the Cherokee died.

3 The Southeast: The Creek Confederacy

The Creeks were the descendants of the Mississippian and Mound Builder cultures. They got their English name "Creeks" because they often lived in the deep woods along creek beds. The Creek Confederacy that emerged in the 17th century included remnants of the Muskogee, Yuchi, Coweta, Alabama, Coosa, and Tuskogee tribes, as well as some Shawnee bands. Some of these tribes did not even speak the same language, but they shared many cultural traditions and were united by the land they considered home.

The Creek Confederacy had no permanent central government, but evolved into a democratic and *communal* society. Like their Mound Builder ancestors, the Creeks lived in towns, called *talwas*. Every town was independent, but the *talwas* worked together to make decisions. In the 18th century, there were about 50 of these towns, which were the main social and political unit of the Creek Confederacy.

How did the Creek Confederacy work? Towns would select a *micco* (or headman), who was part of the central council and who dealt with outsiders. In the 18th century, the Creeks were caught between the English to the east, the Spanish to the south, and the French to the west. However, they negotiated with the European powers for trade and maintained their homelands. In the late 18th and early 19th centuries, their *talwas* were like small nation-states existing alongside the settlements of the young American republic and making treaties with the new federal government.

There were many different **factions** within the Creek Confederacy in the 18th century. Some towns allied with the English, others with the French or Spanish. However, the central council of *miccos* would meet and make many important decisions together, uniting the confederacy. While the European governments wanted to divide the Creek Confederacy to make it less powerful, the *miccos* of the Creeks often played one European power off the other.

After the American Revolution, the Creek Confederacy became more unified because of increased white settlement. The United States government made treaties with the Creeks, but the states where the lands of the tribes existed did not always recognize the federal treaties. Thus, the Creek Confederacy had trouble with Georgia and Alabama, the states that contained their traditional homelands. The state governments ignored the federal treaties and seized Creek lands for the use of settlers.

An important figure in the history of the Creek Confederacy was Alexander McGillivray, a Creek statesman who died in 1793. He was the son of a Scottish father and a Creek mother from Ochiapofa, in what is now Georgia. He became a great diplomat at the end of the 18th century. He persuaded the towns of the Creek

Seminole warriors prepare to ambush U.S. troops
in the swamps of Florida. Remnants of the Creek
Confederacy who hadn't relocated to Indian
Territory, along with runaway slaves, joined the
Seminole tribe, which fought the U.S. Army
before finally surrendering in 1842.

Confederacy to develop a unified foreign policy, and he made the
central council more active. In 1770, McGillivray helped to
formulate the Treaty of New York. In this treaty, the United States

government pledged to protect the Creek Confederacy from outside settlement within its boundaries. When he was asked to *ratify* a bad treaty with the state of Georgia, McGillivray said: "Our lands are our life and breath; if we part with them we part with our blood."

After the War of 1812, the Creeks began to lose power as a confederacy. Unlike the European powers of the previous century, the United States government was not interested in negotiating for trade purposes. Land was the issue. Even though the Creeks had adapted to live like their white neighbors, they were seen as separate from the new country that was taking shape in their homelands. They were often treated badly by white settlers, but they had no legal status that would allow them to protest these abuses.

By 1820, the states where the Creeks lived, Georgia and Alabama, put great pressure on the Confederacy to move west of the Mississippi River. Living within the states was difficult for them, as Native Americans were not considered citizens of states. Many other tribes were caught in the same problem. The federal government offered removal to tribal lands in "Indian Territory" (in what is now Oklahoma) as a way of maintaining tribal *sovereignty* and security.

Throughout the 1820s, the *miccos* of the Creek Confederacy realized that resisting the United States was too destructive. Many of them agreed to sign the Indian Removal Treaty in 1834. However, not all the Creek communities agreed to leave for Indian Territory. Other remnants of the Creek Confederacy survived in the Southeast by continuing to evolve as a people. By the 19th century, these Creeks and the remnants of other tribes who defied U.S. troops had become the Seminole tribe in Florida. Those who avoided removal to Indian Territory lived deep in the inland swamps in regions that white settlers did not care about.

After the removal to Oklahoma, the Creek Confederacy banded together as a single tribe, calling themselves the Muskogee Nation. They were among the 42 tribes that the United States government relocated to Indian Territory during this period. The Muskogee Nation was part of what was known as the Five Civilized Tribes in Indian Territory. The others were the Cherokee, Chickasaw, Choctaw, and Seminole. They were called the Five Civilized Tribes because they had already adapted to white culture before their removal. They often lived in European-style houses, raised livestock as well as traditional crops, and converted to Christianity; some even owned slaves.

29

During the Civil War, the Muskogee Nation was divided, much as the entire nation was. Some Creeks took the side of the North, while others, who owned slaves and had lived in a similar fashion as their white neighbors, took the side of the South. However, after the Civil War, the Creek peoples united once again. In 1867, the tribal leaders

Chief Sequoyah invented the
Cherokee alphabet, enabling
his people to learn to read
and write.

wrote a new constitution for the Muskogee Nation, modeled on the Constitution of the United States.

In 1887, the Dawes Severalty Act broke up the various reservations that had allowed each tribe to hold its land in common. Thus, the Muskogee Nation no longer had a homeland. This law forced each tribal member to take an *allotment*, a small portion of what had been tribally owned land. This had a terrible effect on the power and identity of the Muskogee Nation, as it no longer had the ability to control the destiny of its people.

In spite of this blow to the culture of the Creek Confederacy, the Creeks managed to survive because of their hardiness and adaptability. Today, the Muskogee Nation exists as a political body, safeguarding the rights and customs of what was once a diverse group of people. §

31

A scene from a modern Pueblo festival.
Village dwellers of the American Southwest,
the Pueblos were a generally peaceful people
whose culture flourished before the arrival
of Spanish explorers, missionaries, and
colonists in the 16th century.

 The Southwest: The Pueblos

Before the Spanish explorers arrived in the Southwest from
Mexico, several different native peoples occupied this land. The Navajo
and Apache peoples were **nomadic**, living in seasonal settlements and
calling wide areas of territory their homeland. Far different from these
tribes were the Pueblo tribes. Some may have been the descendants of
the ancient peoples who had inhabited the ruins of Chaco Canyon.

All of the Pueblos had a strongly related culture, but there were
four different languages spoken among them. Each tribe lived in a
village, or group of villages, surrounded by their farmland and hunting
territory. The Western Pueblos, found in western New Mexico and
eastern Arizona, were the Hopi, Zuñi, Acoma, and Laguna. The Eastern
Pueblos lived near or along the Rio Grande; they were the Taos, Isleta,
Jemez, San Juan, San Ildefonso, Cochiti, Zia, Santa Ana, Santa Clara,
San Felipe, and Santo Domingo.

In many ways, the relationship among the Pueblos did not fit the
definition of a confederacy. Although they rarely had conflicts with
each other, they did not usually cooperate with each other, either.
Each community was independent, organized by spiritual leaders who
controlled various aspects of community business.

The Spanish gave the name Pueblo to these town-dwelling peoples. Pueblo means "town" in Spanish.

This diversity and independence from each other was a weakness when the Spanish came. Francisco Vásquez de Coronado, searching for legendary cities of gold, raided Pueblo towns along the Rio Grande in 1540. Many of the Pueblos resisted individually when the Spanish soldiers seized their food supplies, but there was no confederacy or alliance that bound the Pueblos together against a common enemy.

In 1598, Juan de Oñate was given a land grant to New Mexico by the Spanish king. With colonists, missionary Catholic priests, and soldiers, he came north out of Mexico to begin his attempt at establishing a permanent colony. At first, the Pueblo peoples tolerated these intruders. The native holy men at San Juan Pueblo gave the colonists a place to live in a neighborhood in one of their towns, which the Spanish renamed San Gabriel.

However, these neighborly beginnings quickly broke down, and the Pueblos soon had many reasons to wish for an end to the Spanish colony. The primary cause for struggle was religion. The Spanish missionaries who had accompanied the colonists forced the Pueblo natives to convert to Catholicism. The Spanish priests did not understand the spiritual practices of the Pueblos and believed these people were doomed if they were not baptized. Those who openly resisted conversion to this European religion were treated harshly, and sometimes even killed.

The other major complaint of the Pueblos was that they were forced to supply the colonists with food and labor. This was a practice that the Spanish had begun in their colonies in Mexico and South America. *Encomienda* was the system that required the Pueblos to give part of their crops to Spanish settlement leaders. *Repartimiento* was the system that required the citizens of the Pueblos to work in Spanish fields.

In spite of the forced assistance it received from the Pueblo people, the colony failed, and most members of Oñate's group returned to

Spanish explorer Francisco Vásquez de Coronado (pictured here along the Missouri River) came into contact with the Pueblo peoples in 1540, when he traveled north from Mexico in search of the Seven Cities of Cíbola. The mythical cities were said to be constructed entirely of gold.

Mexico in 1606. In 1610, the remaining colony relocated to what is now Santa Fe. With more land grants settled, the Spanish made greater demands of food and labor on the Pueblo peoples. For years, the seeds of bitterness and resentment grew against the Spanish colony.

The alliance that developed among the Pueblos was the direct result of their mistreatment by the Spanish. By the late 17th century, the native holy men had begun to organize the confederacy, with the goal of eliminating the Spanish presence in their homeland.

A spiritual leader from San Juan Pueblo, a man named Popé, became the major figure in the Pueblo Revolt of 1680. Although few details are known about his life, the historical record suggests he was a powerful figure. As a young man, Popé was the war captain of his village. He defied the Spanish by practicing his own religion. In 1674, he was among 47 leaders arrested by the Spanish for sorcery and brought to Santa Fe for trial. Four leaders were hanged; Popé and the rest were whipped.

San Geronimo Mission, Taos, New Mexico. Spanish efforts to convert the Pueblo to Catholicism were a source of conflict.

This experience may have motivated him to organize against the Spanish again, uniting the Pueblos in a common cause. To devise a plan, Popé called meetings in anti-Spanish villages. However, his resistance movement had enemies within the Pueblo community, and soon he had to leave his home village of San Juan for his safety. From there he went to Taos, and, with allies from every Pueblo, he developed the plan for the Pueblo Revolt of 1680.

In spite of careful preparation, Popé's plan almost failed. Pro-Spanish natives in the Pueblo villages informed the Spanish priests who ran the missions. This caused some of the messengers, who ran with secret letters between the Pueblos, to be caught and arrested by the Spanish. Before the whole resistance was exposed, Popé put the plan of attack into action. The Spanish were able to retreat into Santa Fe, but the Pueblo warriors laid siege to the settlement. During the attack, half of the 800 Spanish colonists were killed, and most of their livestock were slaughtered. The siege ended when the Pueblo warriors drove the remaining Spanish down the Rio Grande River to El Paso.

The triumph of the revolt and the fear of a counterattack by the Spanish kept the confederacy together for several years afterward. During this time, Pueblo holy men urged the Pueblo natives to give up European goods and habits. Under Popé's leadership, they held rituals to "unbaptize" the converts to Christianity and urged a return to the old ways. Unfortunately, Popé let his success go to his head and had those who opposed him killed. Popé didn't enjoy his power for long, and after his death in 1684, the Pueblo alliance collapsed.

In 1692, the Spanish returned in force and were able to reoccupy the region. Only the most western Pueblos of the Hopi were not part of the reconquest. This time, the Spanish learned from their past mistakes and did not try to violently impose their culture again. The Spanish and the Pueblo peoples learned how to live alongside each other.

Under Spanish rule, the people of the Pueblos had to give up some of their independence. They became subjects of the Spanish king, and they were baptized at birth and attended Catholic Mass. However, they also maintained their traditional spiritual ceremonies. For their part, the Spanish did not interfere with Pueblo leadership, and Pueblo towns continued to be governed by traditional clan leaders and holy men.

Eventually, the Spanish began to rely on the Pueblos as allies against the nomadic Indian tribes, such as the Apache, Navajo, and Comanche. The long-term consequence of reconquest by the Spanish was that the Pueblos made political decisions independently. Their rural villages functioned like states. When the United States took control of this territory from Mexico in the 1840s, the Pueblos were allowed to remain in their homelands. As a result, they avoided the economic problems that other reservations had in the 19th century.

At the beginning of the 20th century, the old confederacy united once again against an outside threat. Elected members from every Pueblo formed the All Pueblo Council in 1921. "We must unite as we once did before," said one of the leaders. Together, the old confederacy opposed a Senate bill, called the Bursum Bill, that threatened to give Pueblo lands to non-Indians and proposed to limit Pueblo religious practices. This was the first time the Pueblos had united for political purposes since 1680. Their efforts led to the defeat of the bill in 1922.

Although fiercely independent, the Pueblo people have continued to support each other in modern times. They band together for political influence and economic purposes while maintaining the individuality of each Pueblo community. ⑤

39

NATIVE AMERICAN LIFE

Glacier National Park, Montana. At the end of the
19th century, the Blackfeet Confederacy, which had
long resisted signing treaties that would force it to
give up land, finally ceded this and other territory to
the United States.

5 The Great Plains and High Plateau: The Blackfeet Confederacy

The Blackfeet Confederacy included the Blackfeet (Siksika), Blood (Kainah), Piegan (Pikuni), and Small Robe tribes. Blackfeet is an English term, used because these tribes used to dye their moccasins black. In their tribal language, the Blackfeet call themselves *Amskapi Pikuni*. Although their wanderings often separated the confederacy, these tribes shared similar customs and language. They often intermarried and had many family connections. The confederacy came together to celebrate traditional ceremonies or to defend each other against common enemies.

Some archaeological evidence suggests that these tribes lived in their homeland in the upper Missouri River region for thousands of years. Other scholars believe these tribes were originally village-dwelling tribes in Minnesota who moved onto the Plains. They may have been displaced by Eastern tribes moving west or dislocated by colonialists, or they may simply have moved in pursuit of the furs that were part of their livelihood. By the middle of the 18th century, the peoples of the Blackfeet Confederacy had horses, and they became nomadic people of the Plains, following the buffalo.

The languages spoken by the confederacy were part of the Algonquian language group, spoken by many tribes of the Northeast, suggesting that they were once part of the same group of people. Like these Northeastern tribes, the tribes of the confederacy were ruled by chiefs. Followers paid tribute, in the form of food and other objects, to their powerful leaders, who redistributed it to the needy or used it in ceremonies of thanksgiving. Unlike the Northeastern tribes, their only cultivated crop was tobacco, which they used for ceremonial purposes.

The important rituals for the tribes of the Blackfeet Confederacy were the Sun Dance and the vision quest. The vision quest was an important part of a boy's initiation into adulthood among the Native American tribes of the eastern woodlands and the Great Plains areas. The boy went out from the encampment by himself, spending days in prayer and *fasting* so he could discover some sign of his guardian spirit. The Sun Dance was the most important religious ceremony for many of the tribes of the Great Plains. Once a year, in early summer, a Sun Dance was held. With the Sun Dance, the Blackfeet Confederacy would gather and confirm their basic beliefs about the universe and the spirit world.

For the Blackfeet, lakes and rivers had special powers. They were home to the beaver, an animal almost as important as the buffalo. In addition to hunting buffalo, the tribes of the Blackfeet Confederacy came to depend on fur trading, especially beaver pelts, during the 1700s. In fact, fur trading appears to have changed the culture of the tribe. Successful hunters began to take on more than one wife. These "big men" in the tribe had many horses, and they needed several wives to prepare the abundance of furs for trade.

A white trader and an Indian barter on the Great Plains. After the Civil War, a flood of white settlers migrated westward, signaling the beginning of the end of the Plains Indians' way of life.

The Blackfeet Confederacy was known for its hostility toward neighboring tribes and white men. When Lewis and Clark traveled through their territory in 1806, the Blackfeet were the only Native Americans to attack the party. They fought often with the neighboring Shoshone, Flathead, Kutenai, and Snake tribes. Being a successful warrior was an important part of their culture.

Whites shoot buffalo along the Kansas-
Pacific Railroad. Because the Plains Indians
depended so heavily upon these animals,
the extermination of the buffalo was a
major factor in forcing Indians onto
reservations.

The Blackfeet Confederacy was one of several alliances among the tribes of the Plains and High Plateau regions. The Pawnee Confederacy rose to power in the late 18th century, carrying out raids against their enemies to the east and west. In the 19th century, a loose alliance among the Sioux, Arapaho, and Cheyenne dominated the northern Plains. These tribes were challenged by Blackfeet and Pawnee confederations. On the eastern edge of the Plains, the Mandan, Arikara, and Hidatsa were known as the three *affiliated* tribes. These village-dwelling tribes worked in mutual defense against raids from their nomadic neighbors to the west and conflicts with white settlers to the east.

During the 18th century, the Blackfeet Confederacy thrived. They traded furs for guns with English trading companies in Canada, such as the Hudson Bay Company and, with their horses, hunted buffalo on the vast northern Plains. However, as settlers from the United States began to push through their territory in the upper Missouri River region in the 19th century, the fiercely independent Blackfeet Confederacy began to change.

First, disease took its toll. In 1837, a smallpox epidemic killed nearly two-thirds of the Blackfeet, more than 6,000 members. The disease spread as tribal members, who were infected at a white trading post, returned to their tribes. Only a few members of the Small Robe tribe did not die, but this tribe disappeared forever, as the survivors were absorbed into the other tribes of the Blackfeet Confederacy.

Then, the buffalo began to disappear. Buffalo were the major source of food, clothing, and shelter for the Blackfeet Confederacy, but

45

white hunters cut down the herds far more quickly than native hunters. By 1883, the buffalo had been nearly exterminated. As a result, many members of the Confederacy starved to death that winter.

Finally, the territory of the Confederacy's homelands in the United States and Canada caught the eye of white settlers. While the Blackfeet Confederacy avoided a major military confrontation with the United States Army, they resisted signing treaties forcing them to give up their homelands until the end of the 19th century. In 1896, Blackfeet leaders finally signed an agreement with the United States government, giving up territory that eventually became Glacier National Park in Montana.

An important figure in the history of the Blackfeet Confederacy is Crowfoot, a leader and peacemaker who was born around 1821 into the Blood tribe. In his youth, Crowfoot saw the smallpox epidemics devastate his people. His father, Chief Many Names, most likely died of smallpox in the 1837 epidemic.

However, Crowfoot was not raised for peace. A saying in his warrior culture was: "Better to die young as a brave warrior than to get old." By the time he was a young man, he had fought in 19 battles, mostly

The buffalo began to disappear for a number of reasons. Cattle ranchers in the Southwest sent their herds north to graze in the Missouri-Yellowstone region, competing for the buffaloes' food supply. In the 1870s, a new process for curing buffalo hides into tough leather for machine belts, used in the factories of the Northeast, made killing buffalo for their hides more profitable than ever for white hunters.

with other tribes. By his 30s, he became a tribal leader known for his skills as an orator and for his levelheaded approach to solving conflicts.

Helping his people survive was Crowfoot's greatest challenge as a leader. When the buffalo began to disappear and the numbers of white settlers increased in his people's homeland, he realized that the Confederacy was outnumbered and survival depended upon working with the whites, not resisting them. In the 1870s, Crowfoot became a spokesman for the Confederacy, negotiating treaties with the governments of Canada and the United States. In 1877, he signed a treaty with Canada that gave up much territory, a decision that may have saved lives but changed forever the way the Confederacy lived.

Before Crowfoot died, he knew that life had gotten worse for his people, but, unlike some of their neighboring tribes, they had survived. Crowfoot's last words reflect the sorrow and loss he experienced in his lifetime: "What is life? It is the flash of a firefly in the night; it is the breath of a buffalo in the winter time. It is the little shadow which runs across the grass and loses itself in the sunset."

During the late 1800s, the Blackfeet Confederacy lost its power as a political force. It also lost much of its culture, as reservation life and the boarding schools that the government required the children to attend challenged Blackfeet traditions. However, in the past 50 years, the Blackfeet have seen a revival in their culture. Today, over 8,000 members of the Blackfeet Nation live on their reservation in Montana, sustaining their traditions while looking toward the future. $

47

NATIVE AMERICAN LIFE

A powwow in Saskatchewan, Canada. During the 20th century, Native Americans once again banded together in local, national, and even pan-tribal organizations to protect their rights and preserve their cultures.

Modern Confederacies and Pan-Tribal Organizations

Native American confederacies were groups of tribes who agreed to work together, united in a common purpose. Usually, these tribes were neighbors, and what bound them together was a sense of shared connection to the land. However, there have been moments in Native American history when the alliance among tribes was more than something local or regional. *Pan-tribal* confederacies are a big part of Native American life today, but they have also played an important role in the past.

The shared sense of purpose that inspired some tribal leaders to create large confederacies extending to all tribal peoples came from the shared sense of *enmity* toward the European invaders. In the 18th century, Pontiac, an Ottawa chieftain, tried to create an anti-English confederation that stretched from the Great Lakes to the Mississippi River in the years before the American Revolution. However, this confederation failed because of power struggles among the member tribes. In fact, Pontiac was killed by a member of the Kaskaskia tribe, whose chief Pontiac had stabbed to death in a council meeting a few years earlier.

Another attempt at a pan-tribal confederation that included a broad range of tribes and peoples came from two Shawnee leaders, Tecumseh and Tenskwatawa. They began a movement in the early 19th century to unite the peoples of the Ohio River valley. Unlike Pontiac's confederation, they envisioned an alliance that was both political and religious.

Tecumseh cultivated an English alliance and took the side of the British in the War of 1812. However, the young American republic defeated these allies, and Tecumseh died at the Battle of the Thames. The idea of a pan-tribal confederacy died, for a time, with this great leader.

The history of tribal disruption has had a huge effect on the political organization of Native American life. The 19th century was a time of war with the United States over possession of the land. In 1830, the Indian Removal Act forced most Eastern tribes to move to Indian Territory. The strong confederacies of the East lost their power as they attempted to reorganize in their new homelands.

As white settlers continued to pour into the West, alliances among Western tribes tried to hold back the tide. However, they lost many battles and negotiations, and their lands were taken from them. These tribes were then forced to live on reservations. By the end of the 19th century, even Indian Territory had become desirable, and the government made these tribal lands available to white settlers. Soon, the reservation system was under attack as well, and many reservations were broken into privately owned parcels under the Dawes Severalty Act. The tribal alliances forged in hardship nearly disappeared.

Between 1880 and 1934, the U.S. government's policy toward Native Americans was one of *assimilation*. The government's goal was to integrate Indians into the larger society through education, by

Pontiac, an Ottawa chief, parleys with the British. Pontiac had
tried to create an anti-English confederation that stretched
from the Great Lakes to the Mississippi River but finally made
peace with the British in 1766.

breaking up tribally held lands through allotment, and by granting individuals citizenship. *Tribalism* survived, however, and new confederacies emerged from the changing political environment.

In the 19th century, reservations caused diverse tribes to come together as a single group. A good example can be found in the Confederated Tribes of the Warm Springs Reservation in central Oregon. This reservation was established in 1855. The three main tribes that the U.S. government placed there were the Wasco, Paiute, and Sahaptin tribes. Not only had these tribes never lived together in the past, but they also spoke a number of different languages.

In spite of the government's policies of assimilation in the late 19th century, the Confederated Tribes evolved into a fairly unified group, maintaining cultural traditions. They stayed connected to sacred foods, seasonal feasts, and ceremonies involving rites of passage. By 1938, the groups on the reservation had organized a tribal government, an 11-member council with an elected chief. The history of the Confederated Tribes demonstrates the ability of tribal peoples to adapt while keeping their traditions alive.

In the 20th century, many new local Indian organizations formed. These groups struggled for civil rights and *self-determination*. At times, they combined the interests of several tribes. The Alaska Native

Brotherhood and Sisterhood (1912) connected native peoples and sympathetic whites to guard the rights of Inuit peoples. The California Indian Brotherhood (1926) organized various tribes to lobby for more land, better schools and health care, and compensation for lands taken in the broken treaties of the 19th century. The Grand Fire Council (1923) of the Midwest tribes, based in Chicago, called for reform in the way Indians were treated.

Some groups, following in the tradition of Tecumseh and Pontiac, were pan-tribal and included tribes from all over the nation. The Society of American Indians (1911) emphasized that Indians should be involved in their own self-betterment. They wanted to clear up confusing problems with regard to the status of tribal sovereignty and American citizenship. Eventually, this group broke up because of disagreements, but it succeeded in changing the U.S. government's policy of assimilation. The Indian Reorganization Act of 1934 allowed tribes to have greater control over their identity.

The next group to attempt to address pan-tribal interests was the National Congress of American Indians (1944). Its members were the elected leaders of recognized tribes, and they were dedicated to lobbying on behalf of specific tribes. Like other groups, they worked for voting rights and civil equality.

In the second half of the 20th century, the "Red Power" movement emerged. Its members were inspired by the activism of African Americans and Hispanic Americans in the 1960s. At first, its members were mostly young people who felt that, in spite of their

53

traditional respect for the wisdom and leadership of the elders, these elders weren't acting in the best interests of native peoples.

One group composed mostly of students from San Francisco Bay area colleges called itself the Confederation of American Indian Nations (1969). The group's first public action, it decided, would be to occupy the island of Alcatraz, once a native homeland. This group wanted to raise consciousness and build a cultural center on traditional Indian land there.

An even more political group was the American Indian Movement (AIM), started in 1968 to help Indians in urban ghettos in places such as Minneapolis and Los Angeles. Its members ran "survival schools" for Indian youth, helping them adjust to urban life without losing their Indian identity. AIM also strongly protested U.S. government policies toward Native Americans, sometimes resorting to violence, which made the group unpopular in some Native American communities. Today, AIM's major concerns are economic independence, religious freedom, treaty rights, cultural revitalization, and environmental protection.

In the 20th century, surviving tribes reorganized and developed regional and national political alliances. Although the confederacies of the past are mostly gone now, many new confederacies have emerged with the recent revitalization of Native American culture. ⑤

American Indian Movement
leader Russell Means is arrested
during a Columbus Day protest.

Chronology

900–1600 Mississippian culture thrives in the Southeast.

950–1100 Chacoan culture thrives in the Southwest.

1450 The Iroquois League is formed.

1539 Spanish explorer Hernando de Soto lands in Florida.

1540–1542 Spanish explorer Francisco Vásquez de Coronado is in New Mexico.

1584 Sir Walter Raleigh, an English explorer, arrives on the coast of Virginia.

1598 Juan de Oñate establishes a Spanish colony in New Mexico.

1600s The Creek Confederacy is formed.

1608 French explorer Samuel de Champlain arrives in Canada.

1636 The Pequot War is fought in Massachusetts.

1680 Pueblo Revolt occurs.

1740s Blackfeet Confederacy acquires horses.

1754 French and Indian War is fought against English colonials in the Northeast.

1763 Chief Pontiac's uprising takes place.

1775 The American Revolution begins.

1813 Tecumseh, the Shawnee leader of pan-tribal revolt, is killed in battle.

1830 Congress passes the Indian Removal Act.

1834 The Creek Confederacy signs removal treaty.

1837 Smallpox epidemic spreads to the Blackfeet Confederacy.

1887 Congress passes the Dawes Severalty Act.

1934 Congress passes the Indian Reorganization Act.

1968 The American Indian Movement (AIM) is established.

1971 Eighteen chapters of AIM meet to develop a long-range strategy for the future direction of the movement.

1972 AIM members make the "Trail of Broken Treaties" march on Washington, D.C., and occupy the headquarters of the Bureau of Indian Affairs.

1973 A 71-day armed occupation of buildings near Wounded Knee draws attention to the plight of Native Americans.

1994 The "Walk for Justice," a six-month walk from San Francisco to Washington, D.C., is intended to raise awareness of Native American issues as well as the prison ordeal of Indian leader Leonard Peltier.

2002 A Native American woman named Elouise Cobell fights for a $10 billion settlement from the U.S. government that would benefit more than half a million Native Americans in the United States.

2003 According to recent census estimates, there are more than 3 million Native Americans living in the United States and Canada.

Glossary

affiliated brought or received into close connection as a member or branch.

alliance a formal agreement between nations or tribes to cooperate for a specific purpose.

allotment a portion of land granted to Native Americans after the breakup of the reservations.

assimilation the merging of cultural traits from previously distinct cultural groups.

communal participated in, shared, or used in common by members of a group or community.

confederacy an alliance formed for a specific purpose.

democratic having political or social equality.

dialect a variety of language distinguished from other related varieties by special use of grammar or vocabulary, used by speakers who are separated by geography.

dispersed spread widely.

enmity active and typically mutual hatred.

faction a party or group, usually within a government.

fast to go without food for a period of time.

indigenous a native or original inhabitant.

matriarchal term used to describe a society in which the mother is the head of the family and descent is followed through the female line.

nomadic a lifestyle in which people have no permanent home, but move in a traditional route in search of food for themselves or their livestock.

orator one distinguished for skill and power as a public speaker.

pan-tribal encompassing all tribes of the United States.

ratify to approve and sanction formally.

self-determination the freedom of a people to determine the way in which they will be governed and how they will live.

shaman among many tribal peoples, a person who acts as a mediator between the natural and supernatural worlds.

sovereignty the independent power or authority of a state.

syllabary a series or set of written characters, each one of which is used to represent a syllable.

treaty a formal agreement between governments or states about peace, alliances, trade, or other international relations.

tribalism strong loyalty to one's own group or tribe.

wampum cylindrical beads, pierced and strung, used by Native Americans as a medium of exchange, for ornaments, or for ceremonial purposes.

NATIVE AMERICAN LIFE

Further Reading

Davis, Mary B. *Native America in the Twentieth Century: An Encyclopedia.*
New York: Garland, 1994.

Debo, Angie. *A History of the Indians of the United States*. Norman: University
of Oklahoma Press, 1970.

Hoxie, Frederick E., ed. *Encyclopedia of North American Indians*. Boston:
Houghton Mifflin, 1996.

Josephy, Alvin M., Jr. *The Indian Heritage of America*. Boston: Houghton
Mifflin, 1968.

Olson, James S., and Raymond Wilson. *Native Americans in the Twentieth
Century*. Urbana: University of Illinois Press, 1984.

Sherrow, Victoria. *Political Leaders and Peacemakers*. New York: Facts On File,
1994.

Thomas, David Hurst, et al. *The Native Americans: An Illustrated History*.
Atlanta: Turner Publishing, 1993.

Utter, Jack. *American Indians: Answers to Today's Questions*. Lake Ann, Mich.:
National Woodlands Publishing, 1993.

Wright, Ronald. *Stolen Continents: The Americas Through Indian Eyes Since
1492.* Boston: Houghton Mifflin, 1992.

Internet Resources

http://www.ratical.org/many_worlds/6Nations/
This is the Web site for the Six Nations—also known as the Iroquois Nation.

http://www.dickshovel.com/firstnations.html
This is a site index and search tool of issues of *First Nations/First Peoples,* an online magazine.

http://www.rhus.com/Creeks.html
This Web site contains information on the history, biology, and genealogy of the Creeks.

http://www.blackfeetnation.com
This is the official Web site of the Blackfeet Confederacy.

Picture Credits

3: Brian A. Vikander/Corbis
8: Robert Holmes/Corbis
11: Layne Kennedy/Corbis
12: Pierpont Morgan Library/Art Resource, NY
16: Nathan Benn/Corbis
19: Bettmann/Corbis
20: Francis G. Mayer/Corbis
23: Gianni Dagli Orti/Corbis
24: The Woolaroc Museum, Bartlesville, Oklahoma
27: Hulton/Archive/Getty Images
30: North Wind Picture Archives
32: Adam Woolfitt/Corbis
35: Bettmann/Corbis
37: David Muench/Corbis

40: Joseph Sohm; ChromoSohm Inc./Corbis
43: Hulton/Archive/Getty Images
44: Bettmann/Corbis
48: Craig Aurness/Corbis
51: Corbis
55: Hulton/Archive/Getty Images

Cover credits:
front) Gunther Marx Photography/ Corbis
(back) Bettmann/Corbis

NATIVE AMERICAN LIFE

Index

NATIVE AMERICAN LIFE

NATIVE AMERICAN LIFE

Contributors

Dr. Troy Johnson is a Professor of American Indian Studies and History at California State University, Long Beach, California. He is an internationally published author and is the author, co-author, or editor of fifteen books, including *Contemporary Political Issues of the American Indian* (1999), *Red Power: The American Indians' Fight for Freedom* (1999), *American Indian Activism: Alcatraz to the Longest Walk* (1997), and *The Occupation of Alcatraz Island: Indian Self-Determination and the Rise of Indian Activism* (1996). He has published numerous scholarly articles, has spoken at conferences across the United States, and is a member of the editorial board of the journals *American Indian Culture and Research* and *The History Teacher.* Dr. Johnson has served as president of the Society of History Education since 2001. He has been profiled in *Reference Encyclopedia of the American Indian* (2000) and *Directory of American Scholars* (2000). He has won awards for his permanent exhibit at Alcatraz Island; he also was named Most Valuable Professor of the Year by California State University, Long Beach, in 1997. He served as associate director and historical consultant on the PBS documentary film *Alcatraz Is Not an Island* (1999), which won first prize at the 26th annual American Indian Film Festival and was screened at the Sundance Film Festival in 2001. Dr. Johnson lives in Long Beach, California.

Anna Carew-Miller is a freelance writer and former teacher who lives in rural northwestern Connecticut with her husband and daughter. Although she has a Ph.D. in English and has done extensive research and writing on literary topics, more recently, Anna has written books for younger readers, including reference books and middle-reader mysteries.